They Let Down Baskets

Text: Berni Stapleton
Photographs: Jamie Lewis
CD: Chris Brookes

They Let Down Baskets

Text: Berni Stapleton
Photographs: Jamie Lewis
CD: Chris Brookes

killick press
an imprint of Creative Publishers
St. John's, Newfoundland
1998

THE CANADA COUNCIL | LE CONSEIL DES ARTS
FOR THE ARTS | DU CANADA
SINCE 1957 | DEPUIS 1957

We acknowledge the support of the Canada Council for the Arts for our publishing program.

∞Printed on acid-free paper

Cover design: Beth Oberholtzer

Photographs ©Jamie Lewis

CD ©Chris Brookes

Published by
KILLICK PRESS
a Creative Book Publishing imprint
A Division of Robinson-Blackmore Printing & Publishing
P.O. Box 8660, St. John's, Newfoundland A1B 3T7

Printed in Canada by:
ROBINSON-BLACKMORE PRINTING & PUBLISHING

Canadian Cataloguing in Publication Data
Stapleton, Berni

    They let down baskets
    ISBN 1-895387-91-4

1. Fishers — Newfoundland — Social aspects.
2. Fishery policy — Newfoundland — Social aspects.
I. Lewis, Jamie. II. Brookes, Chris, 1943- III. Title.

SH224.N7S73   1998   305.9'6392'09718   C98-950141-8

For Jonathan, my son, with love.

INTRODUCTION

*T*here is a helpless inevitability in documenting disaster. If it could raise the dead or bring the codfish back then it would be colourful magic indeed. Instead it is black-and-white-and-grey art like chiselling gravestones, work that must be done so that a moment of history should not be forgotten or easily repeated, and that its survivors should not be ignored, trampled or short-changed by a world eager to move on to the next day's headlines.

For five hundred years, the Newfoundland cod fishery was the greatest fishery in the world. The fish were so incredibly plentiful that when the Italian navigator John Cabot 'discovered' Newfoundland for the British crown in 1497, it was reported that they could be taken". . . not only with the net but also with a basket in which a stone is put so that the basket may plunge into the water." Over the centuries this teeming fishy multitude birthed and moulded a shoreline society which grew up around it, building the nation and later the province of Newfoundland and Labrador.

Half a millennium later this seemingly inexhaustible resource was suddenly—and belatedly—recognised to be on the brink of extinction. On July 2, 1992, the federal government in Ottawa announced a moratorium on fishing for the species that had filled Cabot's baskets, catapulting more than 30,000 fishermen and plant workers out of work in the largest "layoff" in Canadian history. The moratorium was supposed to last for just two years, during which time it was imagined that the Northern Cod stock would rebound. As this book is published six years later, the moratorium remains in place.

Each of the three authors of this book—a playwright, a photographer, and an audio documentarist—was moved independently to chronicle this apocalypse as it occurred. Berni wrote her diary while touring the province in 1994 with Amy House in "A Tidy Package," their play based on the fishery collapse. Jamie captured his photographs between the summers of 1991 and 1994, and my audio portrait was recorded in 1993. It was only later that we recognised the value of juxtaposing these three portraits—in sound, image, and words—of the time when the codfish disappeared.

We would like to particularly thank Don Morgan and Ed Kavanagh for believing in this project, and the Canada Council for publishing assistance.

We would like to particularly thank Don Morgan and Ed Kavanagh for believing in this project, the Canada Council for publishing assistance, and the Newfoundland and Labrador Arts Council for its support to the artists.

Most of all we would like to thank the Newfoundlanders who shared their thoughts, their hopes and their fears with us while living through this heartbreaking time

—*Chris Brookes, St. John's, July 1998*

the sea boils with silver fish
let down baskets
haul up all that quivering silver
worth its weight in gold
Judas settled for thirty pieces of silver
but the fish keeps coming up
in countless baskets
no worries about betrayal
for us, for this
silver fish

***

*E*verything was fish when I was small: fish drying on flakes, fish drying in Mommy Butt's garden. Red roses smelled like kelp. Squid hung from the clothesline, tentacles waving, delicious torture for a five-year-old. Dried squid with clothespin hats marched through my nightmares.

The sea was my first gentleman caller. Faithful tide, faithful love, never late, never in a hurry. Gifts came regularly. Caplin rolled up on the beach to jump into my waiting bucket. Mysterious shell treasures arranged themselves on shore for me to find, precious jewels I wore in my hair and around my neck. My breath carried the salty perfume of a day spent catching sculpins. Being one myself, I learned how mermaids are created, conjured up by the water. The sea doesn't date just anyone. You've got to have a tail. I want everyone to see my gills but they're invisible.

We fought, the sea and I. Lovers' quarrels.

rage and storm at me all you like
ha ha can't reach me
I know tomorrow you'll be all nice again and calm
wanting to lick my toes
I might throw rocks at you
might stand up to my knees in you
rage and storm at me all you like
do you think I don't know you by now?

St John's, 1991

There was fish in the air when the wind blew up from the boats unloading their catch. There was fish in the hair and skin of my brother. He worked at the plant. I spied on his daily coming home ritual. Keith. My pretend hero from my *Red Fairy* book. He had enchantments to perform before the door to home and supper opened. He hosed the fish guts off his rubber boots. This gained him entrance to the basement. Quick as a wink he whipped off his clothes, stuffed them in the washer and raced to the downstairs shower. All our hot water was used up before the Coming Home Gods were satisfied. My hero emerged princely and pink to take his rightful place at the supper table. Even so, the fishy smell floated up from beneath his Aqua Velva as we ate.

There was fish-magic in my grandfather. His name was John Butler but every child in Marystown called him Daddy Butt. Daddy Butt toiled for Baird's Merchants earning ten cents an hour. He was Weigh-Master. He sized up each catch with his magic eyes, scarcely needing the scales. The weight of every offering was carefully recorded in his green-covered notebook. There was no calculator, of course, nor any need to figure out sums with his yellow pencil. He simply ran his magic finger down the column of figures and scratched in the total. Weigh-Master was always accurate. It was the fish-magic of silver scales on silver scales.

There was fish in church, in the parable about Peter casting out his nets. Jesus liked Peter because he was a fisherman. It's nice to think about Jesus relaxing after a hard day of being holy, jigging a few cod. He could conjure up fishes and loaves whenever he wished, but jigging would be more fun— especially if you could stand right on top of the water! I did not tell these thoughts to Father Penney.

There was fish in my classroom. In grade four history I closed my eyes and listened to Mrs. Slaney tell us our most important lesson: how we were discovered! It was a shock to learn that we did not exist until someone discovered us. Men from faraway places sailed on the ocean until they bumped into Newfoundland. The water teemed with so much fish the boats got stuck and they couldn't turn around and go back. The Portuguese and Spanish looked into the water and knew they had found a special place. The fish were plentiful and cheerful and helpful, leaping up the sides of the wooden ships. The astonished sailors jumped overboard to dance on the backs of cod. There was fish enough for the whole world! That's how I pictured it. They let down baskets over the sides of their boats, and when they hauled them back up Newfoundland began.

Petty Harbour, 1991

4

There was fish everywhere. Most of all there was fish in the water. Everything was fish when I was small.

***

moratorium: 1. A legal authorization to a debtor to suspend payments for a given period. 2. The period during which such suspension is in effect. 3. Any authorized suspension or deferment of action.

I got up this morning, turned Detroit on T.V.
made a pot of coffee, even though there's only me
watched Ricki Lake and Oprah, Regis and Kathy-Lee
I guess the high point of this week
will be the check from U.I.C.

there's no fish by the thousands, no love lost at home
I know I've got no chance of getting on my feet alone
I look into your deep blue eyes, the colour of the sea
I'm going to take this gear tonight, it's all you left to me
I'm going to take this gear tonight, and float my sadness free

"No Fish, No Love"

***

'A Morning on the Water' 1992

Tuesday, October 18/94. St. John's

A line-up of men and women with red-rimmed eyes shake my hand and thank me for telling the world how little they have left. I hope they understand that the standing ovation was for them. I don't think they believed that anyone would ever stand up for them, not in salutation or defence.

Receptions are no places to talk properly to anyone, but I gather up bits of conversations:

"A good fisherman was a good catch when I was a young girl dreaming about a husband. Now my daughter won't tell any of her friends that her dad's a fisherman. She's ashamed of us."

"My son told me being on the package is worse than being on welfare. I cried for three days over that. He's after forgetting all about when he was little and begged to go out on the boat."

"What does that media crowd get out of making us look stupid? They got to pick us clean of our dignity."

The tide went out and never came back in again. Faithless lover. The fish-magic has run out. We are not allowed to let down our baskets. Peter himself could not cast out his nets. What can Jesus multiply if there are no cod left? Would He choose a fisherman with empty nets?

"My brother don't talk to me no more. I'm getting my package but he don't qualify."

"Jerome sits at the kitchen table all day. He got me drove. He don't know what to do with himself if he can't work. I think his nerves are gone."

"His own cousin turned him in! I don't agree with cheating, but you don't expect your own family to turn you in to the government! You can't trust nobody my dear."

This is the opening night of *A Tidy Package*, co-authored and performed by myself and Amy House. The L.S.P.U. Hall is full. The post-show party is going full tilt. The place is crawling with politicians and dignitaries, but the ones who make me the most nervous are the special guests: fishermen, fisherwomen and plant workers. They have been so terrorized by the media, the misinformation, that they were very suspicious about someone writing a play about the moratorium. Acceptance is sweet. Hands reach out to touch mine. Sandpaper skin brushes my too soft fingers. I rise out of the sea of my past, mermaid walking out of the waters of no-fish, defender and explainer of the ancient fish-magic.

Petty Harbour, 1992

I was born in this plant uniform. I became a real person the day I put this on my back and quit school and went to work in the plant. Me! The youngest one in there, making nearly as much money as the teachers—and that was only part time! The plant is the only place I was good at something ... Me! Youngest one in the plant and top of the line! Small hands, see, I'm quick!

I misses it. I misses the plant. I misses tearing over to the bank every payday, lining up in front of them tellers, them all screwing up their noses at us. I misses running over to Reitmans or Smart Set and looking at all the pretty clothes. All them snotty sales girls rolling their eyes and pinching their noses and making their snotty comments about me getting their nice new clothes all stinky. Yeah, well, I could afford to buy their stupid clothes and they couldn't! ... I knew who my friends were, that's for sure. We was all in it together. Beatin' the goddamn quota so that bossy old foreman could go choke from having nothing to yell about ... I never dreamed of any other kind of life ... I was born in this uniform, I grew up in it, I worked in it and I'm not taking it off—not even on the day I dies. Bury me in it ... We got to do the right thing. The right thing to do is wait. We got to wait and be patient and everything will get back to the way it was. The fish will be back. And I'll be ready, supposin' I'm laid out in me goddamn coffin, I'll have me goddamn uniform on!
—Sarah, *A Tidy Package*

Package: 1. Something packed, wrapped up, or bound together, as for transportation. 2. A box, case, or other receptacle used for packing. 3. The act of packing. 4. A combination of items considered as a unit.

my love, you're on the package, you're not the first by half
but you're the only one who's dead, I don't remember how to laugh
I dream about your deep blue eyes, I curse the goddamn sea
sometimes at night when I wake up, I think you're next to me

Trout River, 1992

10

there's no fish by the thousands, no love lost at home
the days all run together, too fast for me alone
what's left will go to folklore, they'll teach it in some class
I'm going to take this gear tonight, the bay is smooth as glass
I'm going to take this gear you left, pray the current's fast

"No Fish, No Love"

***

Sunday, October 23/94. Goose Bay

*E*verything was fish when I grew up. Plays swim out of my fingers, water images everywhere. No matter how hard I try some sneaky fish always swims through my pages. It's in the blood, I've heard. Salt water in the blood. No matter how often I moved away to the mainland, I kept throwing myself back on this shore. Pity the poor caplin. I know just how they feel. How many sketches and skits and songs have I written about the fishery? Not enough.

oh father sails out in the spring of the year
when the ice it melts on the water
he catches the fish then he knits them up
in a fine new dress for his daughter

oh father dear my dress is grand
with its fish tail frills and notions
but it's grown on to my skin so tight
and it draws me down to the ocean

look what you done my daughter dear
out swimmin' like a mermaid
stay clear of the trawlers dear
sing out if you're afraid

Petty Harbour, 1992

oh father don't you be so stunned
it's safe here in the ocean
a fisherman's daughter has one home
the sea steals our devotion

From childhood's hour till now I watched the water for mermaids. Fishermen always carried home strange tales. Sometimes they carried home strange things in their nets. So naturally I'm positively sure I've nearly almost barely glimpsed mermaids, lots of times. I became one myself, of course, conjured up by the sea. Cry salt into salt, throw silver into silver, wish hard enough. Anything can happen. I twisted kelp around my head so I could have long green hair. Long green stinky hair, swarming with flies. Mermaid hair. My mermaids were always stinky. Fairytale mermaids suck. Real mermaids have stinky green hair and sharp pointy teeth so they can bite the heads off sculpins. Real mermaids ride sharks and steal buoys to use as underwater patio lanterns. Real mermaids, like me, keep the fish alive with words and songs. In the folk tale "The Little Mermaid" (not the Disney version!) a mermaid falls in love and wants to shed her tail so she can walk on land and find her prince. A sea witch grants the wish, but warns the little mermaid that every step she takes on land will be like walking on pins and needles. Every step will be pure agony.

It's not so odd to be thinking of such things now. The fish plant uniform I wear in the show feels as right as fins on a cod. My tail. Lately I wait and wait and wait before I take it off and pack it away.

Odd, for a mermaid to come from North West River. That's where I was born. It's always nice to come back to Goose Bay. I'm sad at the sight of all the boarded up military buildings. Tattered monuments to the past, paint peeling and fading to grey. The foreign military are flying fish and they are flying out of here.

More than one hundred people come to see the play. Fishermen and fish-related workers file into the dressing room, urging us to get to the more isolated communities as soon as possible. They mean the places you cannot even fly to, but have to get to by boat or skidoo.

"Women have to make decisions *now*!"

"They *have* to see the play *now*!"

Codroy, 1994

Retraining fever has hit. Why why why, I think, why why why! *Who* says people have to know right now what they want or need? What kind of pressure must they feel, to have to make the one decision which will label them for the rest of their lives? Butcher, Baker, Candlestick Maker ....

eeenie meenie miney moe
catch retraining by the toe
if it bites you let it go

In *A Tidy Package* the character Grace careens from one retraining course to another, desperate to find something to belong to. Retraining has *her* by the toe instead of the other way around. It bites her time and time again but she cannot shake loose of it. She becomes trapped in the cycle, continually retraining for jobs that do not exist.

This tour is a trip through the eye of the moratorium. As with any disaster, it's hard to make sense out of the rubble. It hurts. At the end of "The Little Mermaid," her heart is broken. She turns into sea foam and floats up into the sky. The women of the fish plants can't do that. They must keep trying and trying to survive, even though every step is like walking on pins and needles.

***

Monday, October 24/94. Goose Bay

*T*he weather came down, a jam jar over dragonflies. Nothing flies in or out. Air is silver—wet and heavy with that strange potion of fog and snow. Dance me with the Northern Lights. Whistle me some water. I'm faster than the speed of breath, it hangs behind me as I run. I'm a strange sailor dancing on the back of the Labrador. The fish are so plentiful and cheerful and helpful they practically leap up into my arms. My hands rise up to catch the snowflake fish. No two are alike. Soft white fish fill up my eyes and my mouth and my basket, but they melt away as quickly as they come.

Marches Point, 1993

Tuesday, October 25/94. Port Hope Simpson

I look down from out of the twelve-seater. The jam jar lifted just long enough for us to take off. I wish the plane would stop bouncing. I wish the pilot did not look so young. I wish I knew how on earth we are supposed to land on that teeney tiny slice of gravel they call a landing strip. It looks to be about the same size as a band-aid.

We finally touch down, a sputtery bouncy trouncy landing. Anywhere else in the world the passengers would cheer and whoop in relief, maybe even applaud the pilot. Not here. That feeling of having accomplished the impossible is routine up here. It's also routine to watch the pilot hop out and unload the luggage. A woman named Michelle picks us up.

Me: "Where are you from?"

Her: "Here." (Giving me a look that says, Where else?)

Me: "And your husband?"

Her: "Here!"

Me: "Your parents?"

Her: "Here!"

Everybody is from here. The waitress at the hotel said, "I grew up here and I never wanted to leave."

The hotel is filled with men who are working up in the woods on a new hydro facility. All their mucky work boots are lined up against one wall in the tiny lobby, directly under a sign which orders: REMOVE YOUR BOOTS! I worry about what to do with my own boots but, in the end, decide the sign does not apply to me. There is a small restaurant off the lobby with another sign tacked up: TAKE OFF YOUR BOOTS. THIS MEANS YOU! I hide my feet under the table. The room is filled with big burly men who would be scary if they weren't all in their stocking feet. There is a menu but it does not mean anything. Whatever is cooked today is what you get. The waitress passes me the menu and then states that supper today is turkey neck soup. I am afraid she is going to yell at me to take off my boots. Across the room is a guy who flew in to take school pictures. He is a mainlander. Maybe that is why he does not catch on to

Trout River, 1992

Petty Harbour, 1992

the menu thing. The waitress hands him a menu, tells him he will be having turkey neck soup for his supper and just as she is about to walk away he orders a cheeseburger.

"No," she tells him.

He tries again. "Cod?"

"No," she says.

"Grilled cheese sandwich?"

"No."

He tries to order every single thing on the menu. He gets red and flustered. It's very entertaining to watch. Finally he says, "Well, I, um, well, let me see, what's good today?"

"Turkey neck soup."

"Fine," he says with a flourish. "I'll have that! Now then! May I see your wine list?"

Wordlessly she brings him a beer and walks away before he can say anything else. I watch him eye the sign on the wall and nervously slip off his shoes. All the big burly bootless hydro workers are wearing thick knit socks. After a while the photographer slips his shoes back on because his own socks are thin, black, cotton and monogrammed, and we're all staring at his feet. He's "on the Labrador." What's he doing in patent leather?

Anyone could have seen that the menu was offered so we could all put a good face on things. We can eat turkey neck soup like it's the one thing in the whole wide world we really would have ordered. We can say we like turkey neck soup way better than any steak and baked potato or roast chicken and gravy. Who's to argue? Poor photographer mainland man. He has no instinct for how to put a good face on things. In Newfoundland and Labrador we know all about how to put a good face on bad times. It is very important for your dignity and your hope. One of the most heartrending things about the moratorium is that there seems to be an unwritten law that people be denied their good face. The rest of the world wants to see us pitiful. No menu so you can have good face. No pretending you have choices even though you really do not.

Tonight's show is in the school gym which is not attached to the school. For some reason it is attached to the town hall. Entire families come and everything is festive! It is a genuine treat for them to see a live show and that makes it a genuine treat to perform for them. Little kids sit up front and eat chips and bars and candies and drink cokes. I have to bellow out my lines over the munching and crunching and rattling. I am not offended. I know that for them it is just the

Conception Bay, 1993

same as watching a video. The compliment is that they are comfortable enough to snack and chat about the interesting bits.

The town hall has the dusty smell and feel of an old, long closed up space. Only a few offices are being used. The TAGS office (The Atlantic Groundfish Strategy Program) is barely a cubbyhole. Up and down a corridor tiny bits of paper are tacked on the wall. Retraining notices: truck driver, penitentiary worker, home care worker, hair stylist. Every tiny tacked up piece of paper represents a move away from "Here." The roads are full of ruts and potholes, but it doesn't matter. People travel by skidoo during the long winter months. There's no road out of town. What would a retrained truck driver do? People here take care of their own. What would a retrained home care worker do? All those bits of paper—wallpaper of cruel jokes.

Many houses aren't finished off with clapboard, vehicles are much the worse for wear, and there is no work. These are not the blessings that count in a community like this. The blessing is the community itself. "Here" is the most important place on earth for these people. They cannot leave. I christen thee Port Here. You are here. Everyone here is married to someone from here. One person for each person. What happens if someone gets left over and does not have anyone? It gets dark here in "here." No ambient man-made light at night. The sky, water and land merge into one pitch-black canvas. No wonder that "here" is all the world. When it is this black and there is no way out, it is so good to be "here" and to belong. No one gets left over. Everyone belongs to everyone.

A few of the men still fish crab but, since the moratorium, most haven't fished at all. Still, the wives all refer to their men as fishermen. Everyone is still very clear that they are what they were, and always will be. The "Improving Our Odds" class did not work out very well in this community. Why try to figure out what you want to be when you already know who you are? The A.B.E. (Adult Basic Education) class wasn't popular either. There's a whole other definition of "smart" that A.B.E. can't touch. Read the lay of the land. Memorize the caribou trail. Skin a rabbit, one-two-three. Smile at the kids even though your pockets are empty. Do your adding and subtracting over the stack of bills on the kitchen table.

The government tells people to retrain and move, talks about it like ... pass the salt. As if anyone in their right mind would leave their house, the only thing they own free and clear in this world. Everyone takes care of everyone. As if you would up and move away and leave your

Shoal Bay, 1992

parents, or your brother-in-law, or the old widow down the road. One person can't stop caring because then, everyone would.

People are frightened. They do not want to be "retrained" or "re" anything because then they would no longer be able to see themselves clearly as what they were, what they are.

***

Are you trying to tell me I'm nothing now? I don't count no more? There's no me any more and no Teoph and no life? That's what you're saying. Wipe the blackboard clean, like we don't exist no more, so we all got to get retrained and redone and remade, doing stuff that's beneath us too. Tell me it's not beneath us!

Me and Teoph got the gear and the boat. That's just the same as family. We met at the plant. We got married on the boat he named after me, the "Sarah's Smile." This is what our whole marriage is about. You don't turn your back on that, not because of one little glitch!

The fish can't be all gone. They're just gone away somewhere else for a little while. They're gone on a little holiday somewhere, I don't know! How can there be no more fish? No more fish in all that big water! That's like saying there's no more birds in the sky!
—Sarah, *A Tidy Package*

***

Wednesday, October 26/94. Mary's Harbour/Lodge Bay

I can touch the sky. Whistle down the Northern Lights. Here they come. I sit on a rock. I shiver with cold, or is it the rock that shivers? Rock and me shiver together, wrapped in the vast black shawl of the night sky. There is the Little Dipper. Over there is the Big Dipper. Over further is the Mermaid. People call it the Milky Way but I know it is the big swoosh of a mermaid's tail. Rock and me watch the northern lights dance on the water, an ancient jig in yellow, now red, now blue. My mermaid hair is tundra. The tide nudges the tied up boats, come and play, come and play! The boats sit, mournful hounds, chained up, waiting for master to come back.

Makkovik, 1994

Empty nets do not mean idle hands. Some battle inactivity doing endless volunteer work, or politics, darts, bingo. There are others, though. The silent ones. The shadow people. Like Sarah in the play, some sink in grief. Sarah stays in her house all day. She keeps vigil for the fish. Her hands are not idle. They are still, but ready. Ready for the work to begin again.

The TAGS officer here is a powerhouse. Dorothy is a petite young woman who used to be a fisherwoman. I bet she could make the nets rise up out of the water just by looking at them with her fierce black eyes. She has an intensity that helps her cope with more than two hundred clients and she helped *every single one* of them fill out their papers and applications. Nothing is too much trouble for her. The government sends out forms for this and forms for that and forms for the forms about the forms. The strong and calloused hands of the fishery know everything about hard work, but do not always know how to read and write. Dorothy knows how to protect the strong and calloused hands of her community. She knows all about having good face.

I made my mark on the world
that's my boat you see over there
six hands on board when times were good
paid them all before I paid myself
I made my mark on this town
that's my home you see over there
built it from the ground up, me and a few buddies
we built the church too
I made my mark on more than I ever dreamed
but I can't make my mark
on this piece of paper

Dorothy dreams. She wants to go to university. She wants to be a social worker. She believes she can return to Here and keep her town alive. She works at the TAGS office but after that ... nothing. No work.

Her family, husband and child, of course, are all from Here. She tells me there is little hope for the future, but she works fearlessly to slay that truth. Little Hope is a dragon and she is a dragon slayer. My bets are on her. She is smart.

Little Heart's Ease, 1994

26

I want to ask why she and her husband are building a huge new home. They are building it, literally, with their very own hands. She is proud and joyful because the windows, fixtures and furniture are all being brought in special by boat, at considerable cost. First I think that they are building themselves a gilded cage which will trap them here. The beauty of their belief changes my mind. My life is valid. My town is real. My future is my own. The day to day goals of putting in *this* window, hammering in *that* nail, *this* beautiful carpet will be laid *tomorrow*; these are the things which reinforce the belief that this place is worthwhile and these people are worthwhile. Good face. Besides, if you say you have no future, then you are dead.

Little is finished or polished here in the way most of us expect. No neat little manicured anythings. Rocks and sand rule. Roads are cavernous potholes. Cars are beat to shit. These are not bad things, these are inconsequential things. Anything shiny or new must be found inside of people. There is such hope that the nearby Battle Harbour historic restoration site will become a successful tourist attraction. Everything in this place is a paradox. Disrepair. Disrepair. Disrepair. Despair.

Bella is a waitress at the hotel. She is very unhappy. She was a fisherwoman. Now she tends tables without letting on that every step she takes is like walking on pins and needles.

"I was a fisherwoman," she says with pride; then, "Would you like gravy with your fries?"

She tells me that the fisherwomen were the first to be shifted to part-time by the government, thus the first to be squeezed out. Somehow she qualifies for the "package" but her husband does not. So. She will not take compensation because he cannot. It is a matter of face. Saving face. It's not the same thing as putting a "good" face on things, but "saving" face is also very important. Now she works sixteen hours a day at minimum wage as a waitress. FDO asked her once, when she was trying to stop them from downgrading her to part-time fishing, "And just *where* are your kids while you're out on the water!" They made it sound like a woman being out on the water was the same thing as being out on a drunk or something. No respect. She wanted to say, "And just where are *your* kids while you're holed up in that stupid office all day long! Tsk tsk!" Make no wonder that no one wants to do what the government tells them to.

Shame is coming down like the weather. Jam jar over dragonflies.

I am a place. A place where people can laugh and cry and grieve and be angry. A place where pride can be shown. Listen and write. That's all it takes. I understand, which means that another

Makkovik, 1994

28

person after me might understand, and then another person after that, and another and another. One person at a time is how we might survive this.

***

I put on your old sweater, you'd laugh at it on me
eight years ago this weekend, is when you were lost at sea
I thought it all meant something, the plant filled the days for me
but now my love it's all shut down, they still won't leave us be

no fish by the thousands, no love lost at home
I know there's no chance of me getting on my feet alone
so I look into your deep blue eyes, they're the colour of the sea
I'm going to take this gear, it's what you left to me
I think I'm going take this gear, I know where you'll be

"No Fish, No Love"

***

It's a trick! They're trying to lock us out! They're trying to lock us out of what we deserve. You might think no one cares about you now, but do you think they'll care more about some unemployed home care worker? What are you going to get upgraded to? Your grade nine! Where is all the jobs coming from, for upgraded home care fish plant workers who got their grade nine!
—Sara, *A Tidy Package*

***

'Shared Isolation' 1992

Thursday, October 27/94. St. Anthony

*A*s I pass through the ruination of a province, I become more and more frightened. Every night on stage my character Sarah says, "You don't know how many times I'm so tempted to just get in the boat, sail out the harbour and not come back." I look out at the audience, into the eyes of someone who wants to do just that.

The funniest scene in the play is the one where Grace is retraining to be a hairdresser. She practises on her sister, Sarah, giving her a perm, a colour and a beauty mud mask all at the same time. The result is a fried poodle matted mess. Amy and I have the best time doing that scene. I wear a wig just for that scene, of course, but sometimes I don't have it pinned on tightly enough and it starts slipping around while she's trying to put the rollers in. It's everything we can do not to laugh.

Unfortunately, reality is not so funny. The hairdressers here live on the edge of ruin. The first crops of retrained hairdressers have now eaten into the market so much that *none* of them can earn a living. It's the same in many towns. There are beauty salons everywhere—in basements, spare rooms, laundry rooms, garages. It's not the fault of the women. They thought they were doing something good for themselves. Ottawa must think we grow our hair awfully fast down here.

I see some people who go out and drink quickly to get drunk. Then the sniping starts. Snipe snipe snipe. So-and-so is on the package even though he doesn't qualify; so-and-so has been waiting for his check for months; so-and-so is lost in the computer; so-and-so said such and such. No fish, no love. Can we love ourselves now?

One of the TAGS people in this community told me it was *not* in her job description to *help* in any way, my god, *putting up posters*. Out of the question. Bye now! It is incidental to her that this tour is funded in part by TAGS to specifically address women's issues. Women are lost in the maze of the moratorium. We gathered up their stories and concerns, knit them into a play, gave them a chance to be heard over the roar of the ocean. The woman at the TAGS office doesn't care. I'd like to bite her sculpin head off with my mermaid teeth. It is rare these days to

'Caplin'

hear someone from outside the fishery say anything good about the fishery or the package or retraining—or the people. Greyness seeps into us all. We're steeping in a sad tea. Where is happiness?

One woman wants to leave St. Anthony. She has little work but she can't leave because she can't sell her house. There is no one to buy it. Soon the bank will foreclose, and they will have her empty house and she will have nothing.

One woman wants to leave St. Anthony. She lives with her elderly parents, earning enough to keep herself in pin money but not enough to have a place of her own, not enough to move away.

The people who *want* to retrain and move away aren't fish plant workers so they can't. And the fish plant workers can't leave because they can't—can't leave their small children, can't leave their husbands, can't abandon their elderly relatives, can't walk out of the only home they've ever known, can't can't can't.

Here, and Can't. You are Here, so you Can't.

***

Lord dyin' frig! I had my scum steamed open yesterday when I dropped over to Angie's for a cup of coffee! Then Trese Kelly nearly blinded me trying to wax the eyebrows off me! Nancy Stooley just about hauled me out through the truck window this morning, wanting to do my grey or something. I hates to go out!

You have frigging fried my hair! I can't believe I let the retraining queen do my hair! You're the goddamn retraining queen, that's what you are! Now I'm going to have to shave off all my hair and go around with a wig on for the rest of my life. I'll be going around like poor old Aunt Kathleen, with my wig on crooked and lipstick smeared all over my chin! Why don't you shave my eyebrows off too while you're at it and mark a black line across my forehead? Oh, I forgot, you can't shave off my eyebrows cause Trese Kelly ALREADY WAXED THEM OFF ME!

The whole town is gone mad. This is the only place in the world where you won't get mugged but they'll sneak up behind you and do your hair!
—Sarah, *A Tidy Package*

Labrador Coastal Boat near Battle Harbour, 1994

Sunday, November 5/94. Rocky Harbour

*T*he school gym is crowded. The ocean is just across the road roaring like a hungry lion. Big mouth ocean. Shut up, we know you're there! Go lie down and be quiet!

I keep hearing a new word here: tourism. Folks have bright dreams about b&b's and quaint restaurants and craft shops. We'll cast out our nets for new two-legged tourist fishies.

Video gambling machines are sick. Take 'em out and shoot 'em. From early morning till late night there are people glued to them, sitting, watching, eyes glazed over, pumping pumping pumping money in. It's a sickness that lay in wait for abandoned souls.

If I ruled the world people could use their boats and gear as collateral against loans to educate their kids, or even themselves. Package money would be distributed as bursaries, scholarships, or child-care assistance. There would be a daycare at every course so women with young kids could go. Payback of loans for young or middle-aged or older people would require a certain number of years work in the community. In four to eight years we would have all kinds of doctors, social workers, psychologists, entrepreneurs—all kinds of everybody, in the very towns where now hospitals have no staff because no one wants to live "Here." No one from away, that is.

Some of the retraining courses are not very reputable. I don't know of any monitoring system or required standards. There's no fish but something's fishy. People stuffed into small, dusty rooms like sardines is just not right. Who's in charge? The province is on one big Mad Hatter's tea party tear of retraining. Change places!

***

Codroy, 1994

Monday, November 6/94. Hawke's Bay

*T*hey waited for tourists who did not come this year. The motel is refurbished in a decor of hope. So pretty, so empty. The owner sighs and says, "Maybe next year."

A big new hardware store just opened yesterday. Today it is empty—empty of people that is. The merchandise is there. Shiny new skidoos lined up in a row: pick me! pick me! Christmas decorations hanging around like kids waiting for candy. Shelves stacked, unrelieved of their burden of merchandise. One time I read about how stores in Moscow had all kinds of fine things in them. People lined up to go in and look at everything. Nothing was for sale, though. It was all just for show. Here it is the opposite. No one can buy anything.

The people at the hotel tell me there is no spin-off money any more. The trucks that used to transport the fish, the inspectors, the service people, the boat crews, they don't exist any more. All of that was the staple of local business and so far there is nothing to replace it. There have been efforts by some to access established tourist circuits like elder-hostels and bus tours. The problem is that everyone else in Canada has considerably more experience in selling to the booking agents at the conventions and junkets. Their presentations are slicker. They offer more, they cost less.

So what in the world do we have to show for ourselves? Well, tonight we've got everything in the world we need! We've got potatoes, turnips, cabbage, carrots, pease pudding, figgy duff, salt beef, ketchup and gravy over everything. Apple crisp waiting in a bowl, hot tea steeping in the pot, and after that a taste of blueberry wine for everyone! We're face and eyes into the jiggs dinner! After a jiggs dinner you can't move, much less jig, but it sure gets your cholesterol jumping.

***

Grand Bruit, 1994

Ode to Uncle Bern

a yaffeler don't get paid overtime, a yaffeler don't get no break
old Mr. Rose is watchin', with his big old nosy beak

we're yaffelin' like banshees, don't even stop to blink
old Mr. Rose is watchin', can't even sneak a drink

what a wicked heat my son, tis hot enough to bake
we just keeps on a yaffelin', the fish up to the flake

a wheelbarrow would be some nice, to carry up this fish
but we scoops 'em by the armload b'ys, don't do no good to wish

old Mr. Rose is watchin', Scrooge got nothin' on that man
he's watchin while we're yaffelin', as fast as ever we can

a yaffeller gets ten cents an hour, but we never sees no cash
we gets it in a barter note, now buddies, there's the catch

trade it in for baccy, or some lassie for your tea
but don't go askin' for no money, 'cause Baird's will not agree

old Mr. Rose don't hold no truck, with pay me what you owes me
some quick he'll be to say straight back, tis ye that should pay we

a yaffeler gets to laughin', when his day is finally done
he heads home to his family, to have a bit of fun

old Mr. Rose can go to hell, one yaffel at a time
the one thing Baird's will never own, is the yaffeler laughilin kind

***

Gaskiers, 1993

*F*ish-magic at the height of its powers was still a formidable gift. A good day meant a day of the hardest kind of labour. Uncle Bern worked at Baird's too, back before I was born. The schooners sailed in from all over the world—the Portuguese, the Danes—the lot of them rolling in like pregnant women, heavy with their catch. Baird's had a three-masted schooner called *The Tishie*. The merchants owned everything from boats to souls. Uncle Bern and the rest of the men unloaded the boats with their bare hands. The fish came up by the yaffel, the armload. One fellow in the hold passed up an armload to another fellow on the deck who passed it on to another fellow on the wharf who passed it on ... up to the flakes where it was spread out to dry. Yaffelin'.

I don't imagine there could be an opera house or fancy theatre that would ever thrill me like a high school gym. We don't have proper lights or sound equipment or an expensive set. We've just got ourselves, a few bits and pieces, and our wonderful backdrop painted by Gerry Squires. All we need is a place for people to sit and a piece of floor to perform on. I love to see the audience swarm in, never sitting too far up front at first. After all, who knows what actors are like? You don't want to get too close. They might be dangerous. After the first act there is a short intermission. The gap between us and them disappears. The people move as close as possible to the stage, to the story. They become a part of it. Afterwards we are surrounded by a sea of faces, helping hands, children wanting autographs, offers to come for tea or a mug-up. Tonight the front row was entirely filled with fish plant workers. Every woman's face a flower.

Displaced: this is my new word. I puzzle over it, turn it around in my mouth like hard candy. Displaced. Canada in 1994 and we have a new *displaced* people. Displaced. Displeasing, too?

I visited a retraining class today. The class is supposed to help displaced people determine what would be the best new career for them. It is just like in high school when we had to fill out those silly questionnaires on our likes and dislikes. Fourteen women and one man sit, hands folded on their desks. The women all refer to their husbands as fishermen, although they no longer fish. They refer to themselves as nothing, as in: "I don't do nothing now." For a class

Petty Harbour, 1992

project some of them are going to write me a letter. They have been through four weeks of a twelve week course and they feel O.K.—brave, scared—excited enough to write a letter. How does someone who is only just learning to write a letter decide what "career" is best for her? I think the women like the coming together of the class. It brings a routine to daily living, a sense of doing something.

The instructor of the course asked me if I knew anything about the computers they are supposed to be training on. No one, not even him, knows much about how they work. I watched the women's hands. Hands that could handle the sharpest knife at the speed of lightning, hands that could make short work out of the biggest kind of fish, red and cracked hands of unbelievable strength, hands now tentative and fearful in front of the computer keyboard.

A woman asks me how I got to be a writer and an actor. How did I get to be on T.V. How did I get to be me. I don't know.

***

I'm not goin' in to no self-help improvement class. What odds about their "Improving Your Odds!" I'm not goin' in there. I can't talk right in front of people the way you can Gracie. I can't do it. I just can't. Sure, you goes into that classroom, and everybody got to sit around in a circle, and they goes around and one by one you got to say your name!
— Sarah, *A Tidy Package*

***

Wednesday, November 8/94. Daniel's Harbour

*H*ow did I get to be me? All that confounded fish-magic for one thing. Daddy Butt, for another. He was Weigh-Master. He was a writer, a poet, a comedian. He wrote up his plays and skits and songs and went all around everywhere putting off concerts. When people saw him walking into town, or saw him rowing into the harbour in his dory, they ran for their fiddles and accordions. Everybody wanted to be on stage with Daddy Butt. He was famous in

Hopedale, 1994

his day but he never had his name wrote down. "He never had his name wrote down." That's what the people who remember him tell me now. He never had his name wrote down in history books or chronicles or newspapers, so the memory of him and what he gave to Newfoundland is nowhere for posterity. Except in me. "You takes after your grandfather," they tell me now. John Butler. I write his name down. Thank you, Daddy Butt, for the gift of me.

The mine here closed down in '90. Now the fishery is gone too. I have met Lazarus. He is a Newfoundlander.

A grade twelve student weeps. "I want to be a vet but I don't think I'm going to make it through this year." The wind is sucked out of me at the realization that she is not talking about her grades. She is talking about her will to live. Her parents are desperate. There is no future. There is no hope. Children will not sit next to their parents, as if the failure might rub off. Parents search for strength in raised voices, loudness, anger. Shadow people everywhere.

Someone tried to renovate the motel here by building bits and pieces onto it willy-nilly. The money must have run out suddenly because none of the new bits and pieces are finished. The only thing that works properly in the whole place is the video gambling machine in the bar.

The word "tourism" is not useful here. In a few years visitors will drive through our ghost towns and puzzle over the remains. We are already as mysterious and remote as the pyramids. Visitors might look at grey houses with curtains still hanging in the windows and wonder who used to live there and where they all went. What strange secret spirited us away? Did we disappear into thin air, like the souls on the *Marie Celeste*? Who will honour the vanished ones? Who will remember the unemployment lines long as funeral processions? Who will sing about being swallowed alive into the welfare whale belly? Will someone write our names down?

Resettlement House

my house sailed in on the water
on barrels and logs
my house sailed in chimney and all
happy as a boat
to be a house
that can float
row row row your house?

Port au Choix, 1992

46

my house rolled up the beach
on barrels and logs
my house rolled up curtains and all
happy old soul
to be a house
that can roll
see house, see house roll!

my house plopped into place
on barrels and logs
my house plopped, back porch and all
happy at last
to be a house on the grass
sit stay heel
nice house

my house dreams too much
about barrels and logs
my house dreams, attic and all
don't sleep in my house
it might creep to the water
runaway house

People float and sink, too. Many towns have only a nursing station. Many towns share one doctor. So. If people are depressed, what can they do about it? Who do they talk to? Who helps them?

***

St. Mary's Bay, 1992

Thursday, November 9/94. Cowhead/Parson's Pond

*T*he ocean taps on my window. I sit in my hotel room, minding my own business. I pretend not to see the water spying on me. Lech. It's so close I can open my window and spit into it if I want to.

This busy little town does not appear to mourn the empty fish plant too much. The hotel here is newly redone. It has a huge bar, line-dancing once a week, glamorous lobby and a restaurant so cleverly built that it seems to be sitting on the lap of the bay. A swimming pool squats on the narrow strip of beach between us and the sea. Swimming pool, ocean, shoulder to shoulder.

The people who own and operate this hotel used to own the fish plant. One of the daughters tells me that the plant killed their father, who died of a massive coronary at forty-seven. He owned several plants up and down the coast and worked hard until his death, when his sons took everything over. As far as they're concerned, they got their money and then got out while the getting was good. So now they own this hotel and just bought another one down in Port-aux-Basque. They have no sentimental attachment whatsoever to the fishery. The tourist season was good and their hotel brings a lot of business to town.

It's too bad everyone can't have a happy ending. I expect the people who used to work at the plant have hardships, but a spirit still shines here.

The empty fish plant and the new swimming pool tell an interesting story about the sea. You can't fish in it and you can't swim in it. All it is good for any more is looking at. Lion in a zoo. What should we feed it?

Every community worries over its young. Teachers find themselves on the front lines of violence. Kids act out, act up, act differently than before.

One young boy told me he plans to write for television someday, but not in Newfoundland. Somewhere important!

A grade twelve student twirled around to show me her suede vest with fringes and silver buckles. She made it herself. She is her own advertising agency, wearing her creations to school. If you like what you see just place your order! She plans to pay for her university this way.

Port au Choix, 1992

50

One grade seven student shouted at me, "You should write a play about my mother! Huh! Sitting around on her *package* all day!"

***

Remember the day Hilda slipped on the floor in the plant and went to grab the edge of the counter to save herself and grabbed the block pan instead? And the whole pan of block come down on her head!
—Sarah, *A Tidy Package*

Sarah and Grace squabble, laugh, pray, hope, search and sift the moratorium together. They refuse to be a tidy package, neatly set to one side, sent off to be someone else's problem. They are what they are: sisters, plant workers, neighbours, part of their community.

Grace, pragmatic, determined, focused on her family, turns the system inside out to find a way to survive.

Sarah, sentimental, stubborn, mourning her husband who was lost at sea years ago, walks away.

We each wrote our own part. Mine is Sarah. I wanted her to be a radical, to embrace anarchy, to be a fierce mermaid with a big whalebone sword. Curiously, she wouldn't come out on the page the way I wanted her to. Words show up in their own order. Sometimes they allow themselves to be rearranged. Sometimes not. Sarah's words fashioned themselves into the shape of loyalty. "Lost at sea." Every Newfoundlander has heard that, either on the news or in history books. We sorrowed over the lives of people we did not even know. How can we be accused of taking too much when we paid with the lives of our own flesh and blood? Those are Sarah's thoughts. Mine too. Sarah cannot abandon the fishery because to do so would be to abandon the unburied. Empty graves cannot be retrained.

***

Codroy Valley, 1994

Date Unknown, November/94. Little Heart's Ease

*C*aplin Cove, Long Beach, Little Heart's Ease—one tiny village after another cosied up to the ocean. A knotty twist of road takes us along. Road like a song. Sing me to the water.

> *Cinderella's got her rubber boots on*
> *Snow White got seven wharves*
> *Rapunzel lets down her long net*
> *Sleeping Beauty worked two straight shifts*
> *Goldilocks got three bearskin rugs*
> *she'll sleep in any damn bed she likes*
> *and eat up all the porridge*
> *kiss me nice, once or twice*
> *and then be on your way*
> *take your frigging horse*
> *it's blocking off my driveway*
> *try to be nice to Prince Charming*
> *and he thinks he owns the place*
> *I'se the b'y and all that crap*
> *getting in my face*
> *so long and watch your back*
> *don't let my filletin' knife*
> *hit you on the way out*
> *I'm not your kind of wife*
>
> *Red Riding Hood in wolf's clothing*
> *Delilah cuts off anything with a chainsaw*
> *Gretel outfished Hansel again*
> *Mary had a littlelamb-chops for lunch*
> *Miss Muffet don't sit around on no tuffet*
> *she got spider-veins some bad*
> *standing in the plant all day*

Crow Head New World Island 1994

54

'deed I is in love with you
don't sing that song no more
were you born in a barn or what?
get them mussels off my floor
Prince Charming don't get it
I don't need no rescuin'
I can rant and roar
with the best of 'em
so long and watch your quota
don't let my laughter
hit you on the way out
see you happily ever after

Small children are beginning to write letters to Santa Claus. Mothers curse the ads on T.V. Kids will always wish. Mothers wish, too. A new wrinkle appears with every bill. Debts write themselves out on faces. Eyes of fear. Lips tight. Little ones send off their letters to Santa Claus, dreaming Christmas dreams. Mother would sell her soul to make it happen. Father is present physically but his spirit fled, so as not to see the wishes or the fears.

***

Monday, November 14/94. Burin

*I*t's not unusual for the audience to show up at the same time we do. They help us load in. None of this theatre stuff about the actors not being seen before the show. Sometimes we have to shoo people out of backstage so we can start the play. This is part of the treasure of Newfoundland: my hands are yours if you need them.

People seem very confident that the fish will come back. It is just a matter of time. We have just got to ride it out. All is pep and vim and vigour and complete denial.

I walked out of the gym after the show to find the Northern Lights waiting for me. They followed me down from the Labrador. Clever. I've been afraid my mermaid gills were growing

St. Mary's Bay. 1992

over but I feel them opening up, sucking the salt out of the air. God is doing paint-by-numbers up there. He is not staying inside the lines. God is not a tidy package.

**

Wednesday, November 16/94. St. Lawrence

*D*own the boot we go, to where fog is made. St. Lawrence.

There is a lecture being given on the tidal wave of 1929. Things look desolate here, too calm, too quiet. Another tidal wave is drawing in its breath. The fishery closing was just the beginning. Moratorium came down, jam jar over dragonflies, and started an underwater earthquake. The tidal wave has yet to hit. That's truly when the bottom will fall out from under us. The real tidal wave will come when the money runs out.

How will the Northern Lights find the displaced people? Our paint-by-number pilgrim might lose sight of us when we become immigrants in our own country. A culture this strong is more like oak than willow. It doesn't bend too good. I travel a lot on the mainland. I meet Newfoundlanders who've been up there for two years, twenty, fifty. I never met one up there yet who didn't think he was coming home again to live someday.

Maybe we should all get out now. Start the eternal journey. People have got a little bit of money. They've got a little bit of dignity left. Government should be buying houses, not boats. Let the waters part. Blasphemy. This thought of mine goes against everything I have ever believed.

If fish were farmland, things might be different. We might feel closer to our country. But as it is, we are only Newfoundlanders, and it's only fish. What was ever noble about that to Canadians?

To see with the eye of one's heart is the most painful thing. The fish-magic shields us from the real truth, or else no one would remain. Resettlement lifts its head, hungry. It's time to feed that old idol again. Glimpses of the future through the mists bring grief. Our time is receding, becoming less solid with each passing day. A new time steps over us and pushes us further and further away. Further and further away from ourselves.

Trout River, 1992

Date Unknown, November 94. Grand Bank

*T*his town stares boldfaced at the empty water. It's a stubborn toe-to-toe face-off. It's grand.

The movie theatre is failing. Our play brought in the biggest crowd they had seen all year. They sold tons of popcorn and pop and chips. We performed in front of the huge movie screen, smelling the popcorn, hearing the rattle of potato chips. Rows of men with sea faces file sternly in. They sit, arms folded, waiting to see what these two actressy-types have got to say. When the character of Grace weeps for her husband cause he can't go out and jig a fish for his supper any more, stern sea faces leak salt in the darkness. All along the front row leather-jacketed teenage boys are the first to stand up and cheer. "It's my future that's shut down too! They can't compensate me for that!" one of them tells me.

***

Thursday, November 17/94. Marystown

*M*ermaid returns to where she grew up. I have become a fisheries observer, in my way. The shipyard here has just lost its Hibernia contract. We often hear resentment from non-fishery related unemployed toward fishery unemployed. "A welder who's been laid off doesn't get a compensation package." An old adage has been revised: Never argue religion, politics, or fish.

Hundreds of people crowd in to see the play. There's not a seat to be had. People are parked up against the back wall, or kneeling on the floor, literally with elbows on the stage. At least for a couple of hours we're all of the same mind. Resentments drift away. There's no resisting fish-magic.

***

The Grand Banks, 1992

they say I'm going to be retrained, but they can't retrain my soul
they can't retrain the life you gave, when you sank down in the cold
I'm going to take this gear you left, we'll no longer be apart
I'm sailing out tonight sweetheart, I'll meet you in the watery dark
there's no fish by the thousands, there's no love lost at home
I know I've got no say, in how to stand up on my own
I look into your deep blue eyes, I look into the sea
here is all the gear you left, here love, can you see
take hold of all this gear you left, and now take hold of me

"No Fish, No Love"

Foreign ships sailed over the ocean until they bumped into Newfoundland. They let down baskets and hauled us up. We never knew the time would come when our own faces would be foreign over the water.

Daddy Butt finished out his forty years at Baird's. When times were good he got forty-odd cents an hour. Not in cash, of course. In a barter note, good only at Baird's. Sometimes, even though it was your right, you weren't even free to get what you wanted on your barter note. One time a man walked into Baird's and asked for some baby powder for his new baby. His barter note was good for it. Old Mr. Rose said, "You're not gettin' that! Baby powder! You can use flour like everybody else do!" The man went home with flour for his new baby's bottom. You can ask for what you deserve, what you worked hard for, but you don't always get it.

Daddy Butt walked away after forty years as Weigh-Master. His time was up. No one gave him a pension, or a package or a retirement bonus. He was lucky if he even got his last week's wages. It wouldn't be surprising if he didn't. He went out to Stephenville then, and worked as a clerk on the American base. To me, Daddy Butt was always old, and that's why: he never had a chance to stop.

All that silver fish, once upon a time, no fears of betrayal. What we wouldn't give now for thirty at a time, big silver cod. Who's the Judas?

Mermaid, walking under Northern Lights, frets. Was it too many mermaids biting the heads off yummy fish? No one heard the fish singing. No one hears us.

'Old Anchors' Witless Bay. 1992

The fish will be back. The fish won't be back. The fish will be back better than ever. The fish are gone for good. Scientists and government argue. Fish-magic keeps its mouth shut. Everything is no-fish, for now.

I'm getting on a plane. You'd think I'd be scared to get on a plane, wouldn't you? Actually, it's not the gettin' on part I minds. It's the gettin' off part got me shit-baked.

Eric Malloy's young fella said to him the other day, "Dad! You go out and catch the cod! I'll cut out their tongues and we'll throw 'em right back. We won't have no fish but at least we'll have a few cod tongues to sell!"

I'm goin' to where there's no harbour, no ocean, no fish, no tongues, none of it. I'm goin' to Winnipeg. They lives off the land out there. I got a few people to stay with out there, until I gets straightened away. Half of Newfoundland is up there now, sure.

I got me A.B.E. To tell you the truth, I don't feel no smarter, but I can say my name in front of anybody at all. Don't bother me a bit. I'm all retrained, redone, reprogrammed, ready to go.

I didn't plan it on purpose, Teoph, to be leavin today. It's our anniversary. Things just worked out this way. I got too much anger in me, b'y. I got to go make a new history. I won't forget me old one. I s'pose it would've been better if they could of found your body. I used to love to see the boats sail out there everyday. I'd think, you know, Teoph is gonna have some company out there today. Or, today might be the day they brings Teoph home. Some stupid, what? Then everything shut down and all I thinks about is you out there all by yourself.

I still loves ya. I misses you some lot. I dreams about you all the time. I sees you, you're caught in a ghost net, can't get out, but you're driftin' along in the water, still fishin'.
—Sarah, *A Tidy Package*

***

Portugal Cove, 1991